on rapture & death

STELLA VINITCHI RADULESCU

Solis Press

© 2025 Stella Vinitchi Radulescu

Cover image: "Rapture" by Marie-Thérèse Pent

Published in 2025 by Solis Press

All rights reserved. No part of this publication may be reproduced, stored in a retrieval system, or transmitted, in any form or by any means, electronic, mechanical, photocopying, recording or otherwise, except as permitted by the UK Copyright, Designs and Patents Act 1988, without the prior permission of the publisher.

The author of this work has asserted her rights under the Copyright, Design and Patents Act 1988 to be identified as the author of this work.

This book is sold subject to the condition that it shall not, by way or trade or otherwise, be lent, resold, hired out or otherwise circulated without the publisher's prior consent in any form of binding or cover other than in which it is published and without a similar condition including this condition being imposed on the subsequent purchaser.

ISBN: 978-1-917904-05-6

Published by Solis Press, England

Web: www.solispress.com | *X*: @SolisPress

Contents

one / thistle

decor	2
self-portrait with fire	3
thistle	4
lightness	5
red	6
what belongs to us	7
and so we are	9
endless	11
the genius of the eye	12
on being beautiful	13
the woodpecker the brain & how to bury your friend	14
from old newspapers	15
heaven so what	16
landscape mouth & five fingers	17
departure	18
you are almost alive the hour	19

two / voice   : be mine

summer moon	22
the word not said	23
get the facts the News	24
tango (1)	25
tango (2)	26
allegro	27
staccato for the end of time	28
in the breathing of Spring	30

hang God from the moon	31
a sky I remember	32
beautiful in the rain	33
flood	34
the shell all silence	35
here & now	36
September	37
our story to tell	38
in bold red letters	39
picture the language of *lost*	40

three / the winter yes

how I dream the Earth	42
no-vem-ber – never-more the crow	43
the winter yes & to begin	44
green	45
the wall	46
the bread & salt the house	47
postscript	48
ellipse	49
slow night	50
somewhere is winter	51
the rose supreme	52
cicadas & red balloons	53
the daily facts	54
the cross is looking	55
melancholy	56
all the black angels	57
a souvenir : the Earth in four	58
the second day was like the first	59
the passing into winter	60

four / exit plus

seven sins & a whale	62
and who is He and	63
the baby-snake the moon	64
days of silence	65
exit plus	66
mirage	67
a serpent called me	68
flight	69
on rapture & death	70
a bird & the snow	72
crossing the bridge	73
half eye half voice	74
full landscape with no exit	75
insomnia	76
the legend goes	77
the long road to the heart	78
a name afloat tell me	79
wilderness	80
I am the sum of nothing & all	81
looking for an exit	82
we are born from a flag	83
homecoming	84
I built a silence in my throat	85
through your memory	86
intimacy	87
in tempo	88
delirious it has not been	89
they are coming	90
Acknowledgments	91

And there's something of the hazy noise of things existing ...
—Fernando Pessoa

one /
thistle

decor

a perfect creation starts
with no god   I have
the body of another
woman who glances

at me little eyes and
a skull beyond
dimension:
let's say a sky that
covers my face

becoming what I am
saying   and the gloom
of my few words
enters the era of prose

so dense that each
time you see the sun
rising
I touch a body and
it's mine

self-portrait with fire

I am blind I need a flower

to take me

to my house

my face is pale green

like Spring in the valley

let me guess

my eyes :

I walked all distances

I dreamed all

dreams

they should be sparkling

like fire

thistle

thistle   like a heart

a valve

pumping back life: picture

the blood

    the flowing down

teeth sharpening   angels—

this is not yet set up

the threshold

the clownish hour   come to me

again voice

grass

daffodil   land of blue

land of unspoken

time

lightness

Do not go gentle into that good night ...
        —Dylan Thomas

but carve your body into

a tree morning on earth

night underground two steps

to gloomy sky one

to eternity

from root to top the suffering

of light in chambers

small of time and do not

bend in this

wicked wind stay tall

and ready to fly

red

    red is the color of

        my grandmother's

    shawl that was bought

        in Soroca*

    and melted then with the

        war the flooding

    and the memory of flooding

        a river so perfectly

    wrong you could swim or not

        when the distance

    between two dreams

        shortens and crinkles

    and the black hours

        crafted by hand are

    covering the land   untold

    the drama unfinished

        this day

---

* A city in the Republic of Moldova.

what belongs to us

1.

I am still coming

on the road from drifty places

from your womb

your picture illuminates

the room   mother

of all mothers

a candle a drop of silence

in the roaring

wind

be here when I leave be there

when I stay

I am rushing to the center of the

Earth

where there is no earth but flames

spelling loud your

absence

2.

part of your shadow going

East undoing roads

and rivers   what's lost

    came back again

reclaiming the living

    or walking high

on sunny days   four

    winds intrude the

landscape

    all that belongs to us

the stillness
        of the pond

and so we are

Black holes ain't so black.
—Stephen Hawking

1.

and so we are & have

a name

despite being once

black holes

cut off from every second

from every town

we are still playing

with the stars

expanding our little thoughts

beyond what words

could ever say

some lips could even spell a rose

2.

first page was burned

& so we go

not going anywhere

I took a picture in the park

it was all blurred

then disappeared in a trace

of smoke

you look at me in wonder

while a thousand eyes

so high in time are watching

every move

let me paste your smile

on the wall

& to be you & many more

in this world of falling

lives

3.
and I would like to reach you—

all of you with just

one sound

a sparkle that would inflame

the woods

so you could hear the pacing

of time   the wolf

the hauling

: emptiness

endless

      I entered the room   tore down

           the walls

  the wind is playing around with few

         words

makes them kneel

              withdraw

become   right in my eye

        a bird

disturbs the wholeness of the day

    flies & flies to

            no end

the genius of the eye

    the genius of the eye

    is not to see us

    drowned

    in our own blood—but look

    outside & litter

    the sky   all remnants

    colored

    & pale

    small & big—

        we are clean inside & cleaning

        the air

        pass like a breeze

        in your

        yard

on being beautiful

    so beauty should descend on us

    to find the reason for being

    beautiful & virgin

    in its language   behind

                          the cloud a piano

                          blue

                          would tune its strings

                          to human view

                          displacing layers in the eye

    & where to go

    when you don't see the end

    the metaphor that would expand

            & overturn empires—

    forbidden love on legal ground

    I came too close to you   that's

    why

the woodpecker the brain & how to bury your friend

it's all in the title knock knock against

the wood   claim your right to make noises

& holes in the moon   whatever clicks

in your brain is already gone with your

friend   same with me somebody

woodpeckered

my name

from old newspapers

    all the way to my death   headlines
from old newspapers
                   whose fingers
taped them & then
              disappeared

a drum measures distances   five
fingers   five   & no hand to shake

another hand   does the rain know
   my secrets

did I strip under the moon

old houses & old towns are losing
their meaning

   scrap out your image
from the bible   we are not priests   just

trees   stones   —this clumsiness

heaven so what

Different powers make different mixtures.
—Dante, Paradise, Canto II

delighted to see you here so human

on the road

the *mystic rose* behind   souls

that are real

    forever real & forever alive   yes

I'll start

I am learning how to move the pen

from one circle

      to the next

to skip *the eagle*

the fixed stars
      within myself

not looking back   to burn

& to rise

landscape mouth & five fingers

and no   they don't match

mouth goes first   glows

in the dark   see the animal-like

move

slithering away?

it's all about displacing time

the yesterday

the roaming in your brain

blue & blue the forest ahead—

switch then to eyes: say no

to this darkness

five fingers would have moved

the stone

killed the beast—

these are lips that want to talk

departure

my father came with lilac

eyes   here   or   when   what do you

know about space-time

the door was open on my side   stars

right in time   what do you do with

your hands when nobody

asks you to light a candle—

      inside the house

clip-clop the dreams   outside

the earthly life   the lyric of

departure

you are almost alive   the hour

           speaks loudly

      hands shaping a name   your

     name   like a fleeting thing

        lost in bloom

   : you are due for a word

        flower or thorn

summer moon

    summer moon cut off from my sleep

        flashes of dark

    my feet are cold   *blood* is the word

        to fix crucifixion

    silver stars   silver the color of guilt

        the swan disappears   horses

    take over   I am hiding behind you

        seeding snow on earth

            Voice   : be mine

the word not said

    it shivers   chants   unsaid &
    said   wants
    to sleep & touch

       two hands   one brief corpse
   along the page   *I* and *I* again
   so crisp the light that pushes me

beyond what's said   baby beckett close
your mouth   words are stuck
   in paradise

   where and how to find
the name   the name's name
   in the mirror above

rushing to the meaning   missing vowels
dusty smell   dear whoever my tongue
   your tongue

encrypted me in death

get the facts   the News

arrived   the flame returned

to ash

born from a distant father all mothers

around—

plant some trees to make a landscape &

eyes to see

    naked I went to you to cover me

in love   upstairs the spider

    crack crack the wall

a souvenir wakes up

        should I play Liszt

or Debussy   the death certificate

under the pillow:

forget me not they called the flower and

animals were

roaring in a dream

tango (1)

red is red   but
never blue
I am entitled to live

this season
unzip my eyes
and take the view

to higher sky
they curse and shoot
then split

the land   from house
to house already
night

and children wrapped
in rage
my father on the other

side is cleaning
his glasses
from the earthly view

tango (2)

old dreams are
surfacing
in the dim light
of the day   you

are about to be born
the mother of your
mother   flash flash
the amniotic fluid
in her brain

look now at my big
hands   nothing less
than the story of the
human race   there is

no time for operetta
the heart is rushing
to the end
I am here and I am now

which way the words
go anyway   when the
blood smells like
fire

allegro

death has claws rivers

flow   angels have

thorns

corpses have

eyes

come down God and have

some legs

    windows speak

days have wings

    bloody tongue

words so clean

    be a child

wounds are stars

staccato for the end of time

    after the *Quartet for the End of Time*
    by Olivier Messiaen

       1.
    in time of glory the glorious step
    : only once
                   birth

    or death
    I touch my flesh   there is nothing

    there
    the pristine light   remember :

       2.
    the violin   the staccato written
               for the end of time –

    I hope the hangman won't be
    kind

    bars are bars they keep us from
        smiling

    wounds are wounds they keep us from
        crumbling

    this is how we stick together on the page :
        longing

    I invented the word & now it fights me
    back

    a small twig comes to life the cello kneels
                    on holy ground

3.

but time didn't end
              the clarinet responds
& fear flows away
it's time solidified a colossus like you
don't go away my child

              the piano comes
absorbs the sweetness of the air

the smell of the wind the nightingale's
pain

I open the window & hear the noise
    of the earth

a leaf an arpeggio
        the woodpecker
                a snail

in the breathing of Spring

    we built our house in the breathing

    of Spring

    petunias & lilac fragrance

    each wall a seed brought by the wind—

                    first thought

                    first man

    we hung some pretty words at the window

        a street a pole a tree

        and a small sign

        at the door :

    abandon all hope ye who enter

hang God from the moon

    & pray for

    the fruit slowly

    melting

    in your mouth   his blood

    running too late

    to let you live another

    day   the rhyme goes on

        so do the hands

           leaves of grass by millions

    caressing

      caressing the earth

a sky I remember

    to write a poem it should be

    deep dawn or eight forty five your

    father dead from

        the beginning

    you need a pen to cross out his steps

        in the garden and then

    what   I am full of words   somebody

        watches me

    up & down scraping the emptiness—

        I should have seen a sky

    a clear sky I remember   I should have

        seen   a sparrow   a finch

    clouds gather   return to the

        first day

                a hand is writing

                a poem with no birds

beautiful in the rain

        crossing line after line

    coming to see the world the bleeding

        and the flow of light the contraction

the slaughterhouse   skinny words floating

     on the river

ink for a sonnet rose water for the dead

     what is left & what will grow sorry for

my language of thorns everything will be

     future & past you sit on the rooftop

with folded wings   crossing time after time

     coming to see the beginning of life

flood

he was tall freed from

the world   teeth

like scythes cleaning

the field

knocking on my door

I rushed to write

him

down   streets & houses

were flooded

with time

the shell   all silence

        silence
              in a shell   I might be

there   who called

my name & left it floating

      in the air–

the density collapsed   & where

and how I'll come to life
                      again

here & now

    if you dare to be

        here the long

    waiting the whisper of

        years the breath

    of the sea if you dare

        to fall I'll pin you

    on the wall four by

        four & sound to

    sound if you dare to rise

        listen to the stars

    they are praying

        for you day by day

    and door to door

September

there is a road and then

there isn't

I have to temper my heart

to find a reason for climbing

the hill

& laying down skies

seasons in black letters

 a dying

hour threatens us—

however

    September   the gold

    the purple

    hoo hoo the owl

    is calling

    us

our story to tell

what we are is not enough   a duet
of winds on the skin
of history

the dwarfs the monsters sleep
face down   hysteria in flowers
confusion in clouds

we need a collapse a total eclipse
the Furies unleashed   check
the weather darling debunk
the tenderness

the glamour   we are less than
we could be let's clean out
our words
from hunger & blood   we need

a blackness they know what I mean
they who slept under
no sky   curb the number

of stars to see the night in
its nakedness :

time goes unchecked
this is ours   our story to tell

in bold red letters

      I won't die or

           disappear or pass

    the border   burn

    the flag   in bold red

        letters on the map

    I'll be circled by

       glaciers & ghostly

    towns   from top to top covered

       in sounds   : what

    people are saying of cropping lives

        silencing Pluto

    in the sky

picture the language of *lost*

        the language of

  never down to the last sign

     brightness & the lack

of brightness on the road –

    the country that grows

behind you   traveler   with

    no eyes to see ahead

the beaten face of time

three / the winter yes

how I dream   the Earth

a pomegranate with seeds

exploding

into stars   people picking

them up & storing

in jars   let them do it let them

do it

there is nothing else

beyond what

I am

saying

no-vem-ber – never-more the crow

      will come & knock at the door

    the dreamy ground

      with yellow leaves like yellow

death under my feet   absolve the soul

    jumping around   that's how

I measure in yellow steps

    the distance to my grave

the winter yes & to begin

      a life

      the soul like a pumpkin from

      last year

      beautiful & ready to fly

          dying & dying

      and then
                desire   I mean

      movement   scratch the world

      away

      let the dead die

          open the window &

      look outside

green

    green works like

        a ghost comes

    at night talks about

        trees & grass

    green birds & green cats—

        green takes me

    back to my country where

        I was reading

    Russian poets & Dante now

        I remember

    Tsarskoe-Selo where Akhmatova

        ate an apple

the wall

    inside outside around

    my neck   *I couldn't*

            swallow the whale
  bystanders

    kept the world

 in shape   it was at night it was

 a hollow   let's say

 the cripples overslept

 the hour   my ankles switched

   to water then

 the brain on top
         the day prepared

 to take us
     as we were

the bread & salt the house

everything alive

    the yellow

    the pink coming to smash

    the night   the clearing

    throat   the wholeness   what

I can say in tones of blue

against my father's tomb   the bread

& salt the house that smashes

  the roof

who doesn't have a name & wants

  to be named   who kneels on

empty pages :

speak out this shiny day

  we are going

through our own death   from where

  I am I see a falling cross and

butterflies around   deep flying

in no eyes

postscript

do not disturb

the hour

the dictionary lost we

are loosing time

for everyone a day

was coming

we passed the road

: the hour

stayed behind   the

ghostly postman has

blue eyes   the dog

sleeps and the pigeon

is blind
        clip –

clap   it storms

pay attention you don't

live twice

ellipse

      a butterfly just flew

         in front of my eyes

   say it again   a butterfly –

        it was at night

   I was wearing my body   the tv

   running   they killed

         a man & then
killed two

       the other side

   the Central Park   transparent

      people walking

   dogs   the butterfly still flying

     forgotten   an old Spring

 keeps

       coming & coming

slow night

the fall & the rise   doubtful sun –

on the other side

slow night :

they had fixed the stars

finished the cropping   gentle cry

who is it

we stand in front we stand by each other

like trees like waves   seldom

a knock

at the door   hello   the void :

freeze an eye   it will still cry

somewhere is winter

    somebody cries in my ear

    something happens in the sky

    you know I know

    the rule

        who is playing the flute

        whose steps are crossing

        the lines

    I see tracks on the moon

    souls that are weightless

    colorless eyes   *never* meets

    ever

        we are in the era of guns

        loaded with flowers

        and blood

the rose   supreme

    failed to be rose   I touched

    the ground with wounded

    lips   to say a word

    to leave a sign

    of rapture—

    the fire grew from stone

    to stone

    there was

        an altar in my heart

            & people came & went

    around

cicadas & red balloons

    the season erupts in tears—

        parallel skies

    call it green the space between

        night & night

    like fishing stars in the lagoon

    I am blessed with so many wounds

        it's true

    you came in my ear with old tunes

        cicadas & red balloons

    exploding while I am dying in you

the daily facts

        of life

that's it—

    close the window

rain pouring

    in my veins

that music—

     get your slippers

mama

    be silent while

touring the sky

     it's lonely here

and somebody killed

the giraffe

    people get randomly

shot

or drowned

    in the Pacific

the cross is looking

    for its corpse

    we are ready to scream & kneel

        on the grass

    give away words   splash

        the streets with heavy

    sounds—

        I eat dirt from a star

    there is no need for a pause a rose

    or some music

        hateful world underneath—

    let's stop

                        stop here

        where Heaven starts bleeding

melancholy

    Spring comes in waves of joy

        subtract your body

        from time   it will fly

        free of words   sounds

        entangled with the last

        snow   the bird

                on the roof

  another day   another open tomb

all the black angels

        sit on the beach covered
in water and sand   they speak in waves

     caressing the land and open
a sky proclaiming the rain

they are kind
they are ferocious   night grows
   like a plant in their eyes

they could see
   beyond the flesh –

to brief a corpse it takes me down –
   I'll be free of sounds & birds

   shock me with a glitter
of love

a souvenir : the Earth in four

    dimensions   gender   race

two palpable

    wounds   a heart &

a heart   a woman dancing

    on the floor and the

violent *I*—

    I can design a planet or

the moon free from me

    a clownish step &

ecstasy around

the second day was like the first

       the butterflies came late the

    breathing of the sea cut short   is there

      a hero behind the door trimming

moments of joy   we play with words

    like the wind with some

rocks   green night & foggy tongue

    to name a thing it takes

   a life : the chaos split in two

   or five & colored red

or blue

the passing into winter

    alliteration under the bear's skin

        & from outside the noise

    of blood   the changing

        of the season   winds

    caught in letters   but that's not all

        it's not the end

    the vowels whisper   his

        breath absorbs the sounds :

    the passing

        into winter

seven sins & a whale

      It starts with the guilt of

          touching the page   who

  needs letters & signs

      describing Hell

next   comes   the sinful   white

     covering what happened

              so far—

a witch   snowflakes   white teeth

    the white of an egg

 & then   nostalgic the whale

    swallows the rest

and who is He   and

        where to look to find

no answer

    but the question –

he slept his life & then awake

      knelt in my heart as

kneeling will have dug

          a grave—

  some people still are calling

  me   dividing parts

   & sounds

– what do I love & what belongs

to me —   my fingers touch

  & touch your face

and touching

      is the answer

the baby-snake the moon

       the womb in my womb grew

          bigger than the moon

                    voices
grow thin

       beyond my eyes the Milky Way   silence

       like water.
                      like water

       breaking the stone

          yes

       I see two eggs instead of one

days of silence

    a house in the woods
    passing flocks of wild geese   the crimson

    taste of Summer

        a poet sits on the porch

        he trims rosebushes & clouds

        the moon gets heavy cripples the roof

    the Earth feels like home

exit plus

it's snowing in town—

still Sunday

would you come wind

to comb my hair

would you come world

to cover me

in words

deserted hands look for an exit

never mind the future

we are already

past—

however in caves a small light

makes its way

to my eye

mirage

so, we met then one day

or clouds

in the mirror

shade of two bodies moving around

    the unlocatable town

I don't want to talk but words

pop up in my mouth

what should I say or do

undo the night:

    the Summer night   roses & fireflies—

have we been there

or here

in the glow sharing this grave

a serpent called me

      God   the voice entangled in my hair

      humid like humid nights

      by the sea we used to be humans

            once

            spit fire from inside   he took

      my face & dug

      two eyes   I see you now

      with angels

flight

      trying to catch the hour to

          build a house around

     with clouds extend

         the moving floor

     beyond the absent

        sun   who dares

     not to comply

        with time   delay

     the moment as it

        comes   & rising

     up into the void   o Muse you

        stream of life

on rapture & death

    we are dying my friend of loving
    one another   light & shadow   sun
    & stars

    we are guilty of rapture & faith
    even of beauty—

    new species of humans rise in the air
    my heart

    unfaithful child   stop the rivers stop

    the vowels
    I could *be* again and like Medusa spit

    fire around
    we don't pray but if we do we randomly

     kill one another

    words can carry any weight   flowers
    stick to red   — give me five cents to buy
    half of the sky

    gloomy

    as the gloomy eye   we are dying
    from the winds to come from

     the moon

    from our love   did I measure the Earth
    did I call you God

    Rolling Stones in the air   windows
    open

Spring is coming

what makes us to see the branch
growing higher than the eye   some of us
already passed as the hour
went ahead

I can play Pierrot or Hamlet if I lose the

rhythm I panic

seconds minutes make no sense
we are meant to be as such

let's skip time & keep

the music

a bird & the snow

    it was deep dawn in one

    of the worlds   hands

    swimming

    keeping up with the flow

    I was about

    to be born   full sky

    underneath

    sounds

    like empty shells :   let's call them words set up

                  a flower

                  a bird & the snow

crossing the bridge

      o the big world in five cursive

      letters what you can spell

      or spit

          the goddesses of here

      & there running the weather —

             we are running empires

                small tribes along the beach

                the flowered

the forgotten   small

is small

& huge coffins are sold

by the wall of forgiveness   too little

to say
        too much to silence

we are crossing the bridge

looking for the perfect word that

    sits unclaimed on our

              tongues

half eye half voice

    start from here the black hole

    the warm & warming

    particles of life:

    half eye half voice—

    divided in species & stars

    we stopped the killing

    and birds start

    flying and jasmine fragrance

    returns

    to earth

    each other's image each other's

    sister   days pop up

    and nights

    by the river   —update your face—

    the flowing down

    : invention of blood

full landscape with no exit

    I didn't do it   the crisp light by

    itself mounted the statue

    and silence bleeds

    in my throat

    mauve-orchid the color of your eyes

        full mauve like a cathedral

        opens a secret door

    stay on page so you could breathe

    but breathing is a flower with

        sharp teeth   or stop

    thinking of me or break my bones

    and let them shine a stellar city

        under the sea

insomnia

    it's night   insomnia has

its way

to alter the clock

    what remains   a soul unsaid

untouched

wandering around   – frail & sleepy

the angel—

one eye open the other

                closed—

it will be light & one more day

on earth :

    so said the rat of time

the legend goes

      the legend goes about planets and ants rivers

      & oceans a woman swimming

      up & down

      a siren born in her womb

                                  the s a i l o r   spell it

slow

                                  with a hundred ears never

                                  found his way

                                  to the shore

the long road to the heart

    name it   oh wait

    it's already here on the plate

    long screams & children on the road
    a fiesta might be going on

    on bloody land—
    it's late so late how could I fall

    & rise
    from my own flesh   a sentence

    never ends   or it does
    an empty nest fell down from my sleep

    fill it up with words big & small
    blackbirds & songs—

a name   afloat   tell me

        one story
                  two stories

        until you quench
                          my thirst

        going to the river
                  small steps in the grass

        and the serpent
                  will follow   music

        coming from the ground
                        —I am alive

   a name   afloat   listen
                            to the echo

wilderness

    I can't hear you   stuck

  in this wilderness sometimes

      it is quiet

  sometimes I cry   this is a poem

      for blind elephants

  crossing the page   stepping

      on graves

 it smells like fire and a star

      dies in my eyes

  adieu my love   these words

      will burn me

  to the end

I am the sum of nothing & all

        the difference

    between silence
          & noise

    an autumn late or

        the forthcoming
           spring

    the nightingale up
          in the sky

    the burnt cathedral
          in my eye or

    the conclusion of
         being such

   a parody
     of space & time

looking for an exit

some poems shine some

are allergic to writing stuck

on my tongue looking

for an exit   then everything

goes silent

corpses   trees   left in the

sun   on the other

side   light   so thin   the earth

is yours   as you step on

if you say :   *my body*

it will grow wings   I already

hear the trumpets

rising

we are born from a flag

we are born from a flag   foggy
souls looking for
a home
the rhythm of our hearts the melody
of stones

whose steps are blocking
the road
packing death like fully ripe
apples
gloves infected
with life   — keep
the corpse in the freezer or

throw it in the truck   *sweet baby*
he wrote with a marker
on a small bundle   the tall man
with a mask

homecoming

a piece of paper floating

on the river   homecoming :

    museum of bones

some words transcend   free

    blood on my tongue

: a landscape with feathers and

    stars that fit in one eye

memory   : you strange animal

    and the white forest

that follows

I built a silence in my throat

a neverness with feathers

and clock   hard

to erase what's never said

dreamed or drenched

in the day ahead   you sister of the

moon

open the gate   someone is speaking

& flames are rising

everywhere

through your memory

                      an eye blinks

    a letter down the road

            clearing the path to

Ascension   soul to soul:

    lumière   it's

almost summer

    you are rising into—

        this mouth the shape of

   today's loneliness   saying words

     that don't exist

            by evening I became

                one of them

nothing can die now through me

intimacy

      I am in touch with

          myself   lips—

  rouge—the smell of death

      the blue

of an eye   flower   you

    two hands : the music

and under my nails   what's

    under my nails

        tomorrow?

yesterday?

in tempo

     go

  go find the route

    full night

  & stars

  the metaphor in

    your hands

  four letters / five

    building

  the temple

    we are dying

  inside

delirious   it has not been

        said   not being aware

wind dropping down

          stars   write

with your eyes   what is

   invisible   sheltered

here   home-called

   home-blueness   snow

falling on the other

         side

couldn't get through

  the forest of time

     not cutting

        branches in two and
killing

  birds at random

    how cruel each step before and
behind   how sweet

   the pacing into life

they are coming

        the waves

    the hours & the lack of hours digging

your grave

     who are you & why are you

here   at the beginning of the end

            I am full of time unspent

      unaware   too much of this

  too much of that   heart   heart

     who dies once dies many times

    heart pulsing
                      with love

    the fire creeping down

                        : ash

Acknowledgments

The Writing Disorder Literary Journal, Summer 2024: I am the sum, melancholia, the rose, they are coming

Ginosko Literary Journal: Lightness, beautiful in the rain, wilderness, September, hang god from the moon, I built a silence in my throut.

Asheville Poetry Review: looking for an exit

Dark Onus Lit: flood

Molecule LitMag: the woodpecker the brain & how to bury your friend

The Glacier: the long road to the heart, half eye half voice, green

Midway Journal: on rapture & death, full landscape with no exit

Divot Journal: self-portrait with fire, decor

Metafore: the baby-snake the moon

Cecile's Writers Magazine (Netherlands): exit plus

Otis Nebula 12: and so we are

Hermeneutic Chaos Journal: landscape mouth & five fingers

Five 2 One Magazine, Five Micro Poems: thistle

www.ingramcontent.com/pod-product-compliance
Lightning Source LLC
Chambersburg PA
CBHW061235070526
44584CB00030B/4142